THIS WALKER BOOK BELONGS TO:

For Albert

First published 1982 by Evans Brothers Ltd
This edition published 1991 by Walker Books Ltd
87 Vauxhall Walk, London SE11 5HJ

Printed and bound in Hong Kong by
Dai Nippon Printing Co. (HK) Ltd

British Library Cataloguing in Publication Data
Hawkins, Colin
How to look after your cat.
I. Title
823'.914[J]
ISBN 0-7445-2078-9

HOW TO LOOK AFTER YOUR CAT

Colin Hawkins

WALKER BOOKS
LONDON

Which Cat?

What kind of cat
would you like to own?
Should it be male or female?

If you decide on a female
would you like her
to have kittens?

Should it be a long-haired
or a short-haired cat?

Long-haired cats are very
beautiful animals but require
a great deal of care and grooming.

Siamese cats are affectionate
and playful, but they can be
destructive and noisy.

The Cornish Rex has crinkled fur and whiskers.

Odd-eyed white has one eye blue and the other orange.

Would you prefer an exotic cat who can be entered for cat shows, but who will be expensive to buy and maintain, or a cross-bred cat who will be cheap to buy and possibly healthier and stronger?

Nor is there any reason why a stray or alley cat should not make a good pet.

Choosing Your Cat

In selecting a healthy kitten look for the following:

alert, happy nature

clear, bright eyes

damp, moist nose

healthy, pink tongue

sleek, well-groomed coat

strong, firm limbs and feet

a good appetite

Avoid overweight kittens. They could have a glandular problem.

Pick a lively, happy kitten.

Shy, nervous, hissing kittens do not make good pets.

Wheezing kittens should also be avoided as they may well have asthmatic problems or even cat flu.

The New Kitten

Before taking a kitten home, ensure that he has had all the necessary inoculations.

Injections should be given at six and twelve weeks, then once a year thereafter.

Kittens should not be taken away before ten weeks old.

Provide the new kitten with his own basket and litter tray.

Keep your kitten indoors for at least six days so that he can become familiar with his new home.

The litter tray can gradually be moved closer to the door and then eventually outside.

Diet

Do not over-feed your kitten. He is an enthusiastic eater and will literally eat until he is sick.

Ideally kittens of about ten weeks should have four small, milk-based meals a day – cereal and wholemeal bread with milk. At six months, three meals a day. Then, when fully grown, two meals a day. Gradually introduce a solid meat and fish-based diet.

Cats also enjoy drinking tea. This helps to keep their coats in good condition.

Water with all meals is essential.

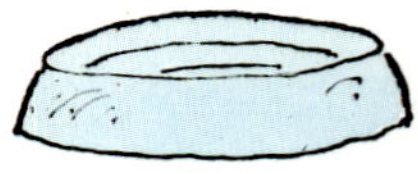

Never put your plate on the floor for your cat to finish off any scraps or he may begin to steal from the table.

Apart from their normal diet of meat, fish and eggs, cats will also eat more unusual foods such as bananas, cheese and cake.

Cats eat grass as an aid to their digestion. It helps to prevent hair-balls forming after grooming.

Grooming

Short-haired cats will largely take care of their own grooming. Long-haired cats should be brushed and combed every day or their coats will soon become matted and untidy. All cats are liable to have problems with fleas. Check frequently and dust when necessary with flea powder.

A cat's teeth should be cleaned once a month with a soft cloth and salt water.

Cats really hate being bathed and so should only be given a bath in extreme situations. Use only warm water with a mild soap, avoid disinfectants, and then rinse and dry very well.

Keep indoors until completely dry.

Cat Care

Provide a secure and well-ventilated cat basket when transporting a cat over any distance.

Cats as a rule do not enjoy travelling, so make the basket as warm and comfortable as possible.

It's a good idea for a cat to wear a collar that can carry his name and address. Do ensure that it is elasticated.

A bell attached to a collar will help to prevent a cat from catching birds.

A flap fitted to an outside door will allow your cat to come and go as he wishes. Although you can have the occasional unexpected visitor.

Providing your cat with a scratching post can prevent damage to furniture.

Nails should be trimmed, if necessary, every two or three weeks.

Sick Cats and How to Recognize Them

Loss of appetite

This may simply mean that he's bored with his diet. Try changing it.

Shivering

A hot, dry nose

Being sick

This may be due to overeating.

Sneezing

Cat flu is fairly common and can be dangerous. The occasional sneezing fit however is more likely to be due to dust or hay fever.

Bald patches

These can be a sign of ringworm or a vitamin deficiency. Or may be due to fighting. Patches on the neck may be caused by the collar rubbing.

A combination of any two or three of these symptoms will almost certainly mean that your cat is sick and should see a vet.

The sick cat should be kept in a warm bed out of draughts. A hot water bottle placed in the basket is a good idea.

Keep a litter tray close by. If he is very weak it may be necessary to carry him to the tray.

Grooming a sick cat will make him feel better.

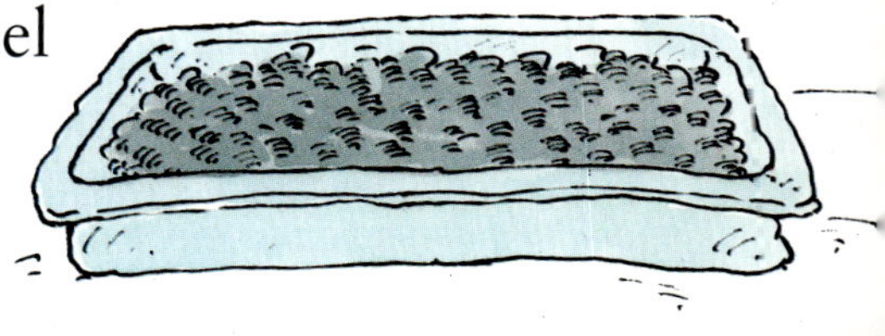

Giving tablets

To prevent cats spitting out tablets, ensure that you place them right at the back of the tongue and then hold the mouth closed until they swallow.

To Spay or Not to Spay?

Unspayed male cats mark out their territory with very pungent urine.

They will also fight other male cats over territorial rights.

It is often thought that spayed male cats become fat, lazy and useless. This is untrue. A cat will only become fat and lazy if over-fed.

When in season, a female cat will attract gangs of enthusiastic and raucous suitors.

An unspayed female cat will come into season three times a year. Unless you are able to find homes for all her kittens you will soon have a very large family of cats to feed.

The Mother-To-Be

A cat's pregnancy lasts between sixty and sixty-five days. During the final twenty-one days she will become very large indeed.

With about fourteen days to go she will become restless and begin looking for a suitable place to have her litter. When she has found the right spot, make it comfortable for her with blankets or newspapers.

Try to prevent her from being frightened late in her pregnancy or she may miscarry.

Shortly before the birth of her kittens she will become very thirsty and incredibly affectionate.

The Happy Event

It is very important to avoid disturbing the new mother or she may carry off the kittens to a more inaccessible place.

A mother cat will eat at least four times more than she normally eats.

At about two weeks, place a litter tray near the bed. The mother cat will then teach the kittens how to use it.

Kittens can start to be weaned at about four weeks.

They will learn how to drink milk by trial and error.

Kittens will open their eyes after about nine days, but it will be two or three more days before they are able to hear.

Kittens will begin to lose their milk teeth at about four months.

Cat Tales

All American tabby cats are thought to be descended from the ship's cat that came over with the Pilgrim Fathers.

Thousands of years ago the cat goddess "Bast" or "Pasht" was worshipped in Egypt. This is thought to be why we call cats "Puss" today.

In Australia thirteen kittens were born in one litter – and they all survived.

Turkish Van cats actually enjoy swimming and will spend long periods of time in the water.

In Mexico there is a breed of cat without any hair.

MORE WALKER PAPERBACKS
For You to Enjoy

Also by Colin & Jacqui Hawkins

How to Look After Your Dog

"Even the most serious piece of advice is made palatable by the delightful drawings ..
If you've never wanted a dog before you certainly will after reading this book." *The Observer*
ISBN 0-7445-2079-7 £1.99

Farmyard Sounds / Jungle Sounds

"Lots of jolly cartoon-style animals... Every child I've ever known loves making animal noises, so be prepared to do your stuff." *Tony Bradman, Parents*
Farmyard Sounds 0-7445-1752-4 £2.99
Jungle Sounds 0-7445-1753-2 £2.99

Terrible Terrible Tiger / The Wizard's Cat

Two wonderfully entertaining rhyming picture books about a tiger who is not quite what he seems and a cat who wishes he were something else.
Terrible Terrible Tiger 0-7445-1063-5 £2.99
The Wizard's Cat 0-7445-1389-8 £2.99

Walker Paperbacks are available from most booksellers, or by post from Walker Books Ltd, PO Box 11, Falmouth, Cornwall TR10 9EN.

To order, send: Title, author, ISBN number and price for each book ordered
Your full name and address
Cheque or postal order for the total amount, plus postage and packing:
UK, BFPO and Eire – 50p for first book, plus 10p for each additional book to a maximum charge of £2.00.
Overseas Customers – £1.25 for first book, plus 25p per copy for each additional book.
Prices are correct at time of going to press, but are subject to change without notice.